Writer's Little Instruction Book

CRAFT & TECHNIQUE

PAUL RAYMOND MARTIN

WRITER'S DIGEST BOOKS
Cincinnati, Ohio
www.writersdigest.com

Writer's Little Instruction Book: Craft & Technique. © 2005 by Paul Raymond Martin. Manufactured in the United States of America. All rights reserved. No part of this book may be reproduced in any form or by any electronic or mechanical means including information storage and retrieval systems without permission in writing from the publisher, except by a reviewer, who may quote brief passages in a review. Published by Writer's Digest Books, an imprint of F+W Publications, Inc., 4700 East Galbraith Road, Cincinnati, OH 45236. (800) 289-0963. First edition.

Visit our Web site at www.writersdigest.com for information on more resources for writers. To receive a free weekly e-mail newsletter delivering tips and updates about writing and about Writer's Digest products, register directly at our Web site at http://newsletters.fwpublications.com.

09 08 07 06 05   5 4 3 2 1

Library of Congress Cataloging-in-Publication Data

Martin, Paul Raymond.
  Writer's little instruction book. Craft & technique : includes more than 300 aphorisms and insights / by Paul Raymond Martin.
       p. cm.
  ISBN 1-58297-341-5 (pbk. : alk. paper)
  1. Authorship. 2. Creative writing. I. Title: Craft & technique. II. Title.
  PN147.M422 2005   2004028845
  808'.02—dc22

Edited by Kelly Nickell
Designed by Lisa Buchanan-Kuhn and Grace Ring
Cover Photography by Al Parrish
Page Layout by Jessica Schultz
Production Coordinated by Robin Richie

F+W PUBLICATIONS, INC.

DEDICATION

This book is dedicated to:

John and Bee, Jim and Marcy

for their support, and for allowing me the personal space to write.

ACKNOWLEDGMENTS

Robin Estrin, for her constancy and encouragement.

Jane Friedman, who stuck her neck out in a new job to acquire this book.

Lavern Hall, who will always be my first publisher.

Lisa Kuhn and Grace Ring, who made this a beautiful book with their design.

Kirk Nesset, the best short fiction critiquer I have ever encountered.

Kelly Nickell, who made this a better book with her editing.

Rita Rosenkranz, who negotiated the contract and freed me to write.

Kathie Westerfield, who provided me with a writing haven when I most needed it.

TABLE OF CONTENTS

INTRODUCTION:
CRAFT & TECHNIQUE

The response to *The Writer's Little Instruction Book: 385 Secrets for Writing Well & Getting Published*, originally released in 1998, was both gratifying and surprising. My little book, adopted by classroom teachers from middle school through college, also became a hit at writers' workshops. While I didn't anticipate so many readers would draw life lessons from it, as well as inspiration and instruction for their writing, the results have been most rewarding. Thus, my little book has grown into a series of three:

Writer's Little Instruction Book: Inspiration & Motivation
Writer's Little Instruction Book: Craft & Technique
Writer's Little Instruction Book: Getting Published

Each volume includes motivational quotes and secrets for effective writing from prominent authors and editors, original aphorisms to keep you focused and on track, anecdotes to illustrate key points related to writing and the writing life, and story starters or publishing strategies to inspire your work when you're stuck or when you just want to try something new.

May your stride be longer returning from the mailbox than on the way to it.

CHARACTERIZATION:

Every Memorable
Character Has a Wart

I live with the people I create and it has always **made my essential loneliness less keen.**

—Carson McCullers, author of *The Heart Is a Lonely Hunter*

When I'm writing about myself I think about myself as a character. There is a ton of stuff going on in my life that I don't write about. If I need to write that stuff down, I write about myself in my diary.

—David Sedaris, author of *Me Talk Pretty One Day*

I have tried every device I know to breathe life into my characters, for there is little in fiction more rewarding than to see real people on the page.

—James A. Michener, Pulitzer Prize-winning author of *Tales of the South Pacific*

Your most engaging characters will **rise from the dust** and detritus of personal experience.

➤ An attentive writer is midwife, nanny, uncle, and undertaker to the story's characters.

➤ Study ordinary people in order to create extraordinary characters.

➤ Main characters must act, not be acted upon.

➤ Use as few characters as possible. Save the others for telling their own stories.

➤ Every character changes the story. Every story changes the character.

It's been said, "**Fiction is life dressed up for a party.**" And the writer controls the guest list.

➤ In order for the characters to speak, the writer must remain silent.

➤ The sins of the writer are visited upon the writer's characters.

➤ Each character must act in accord with his or her nature, not the writer's.

Define your characters carefully, for they in turn will define the depth of your work.

Characters are nothing **until your readers create them.**

Like everyday folks, characters must be in enough pain to **make a change** in their lives.

> Develop empathy toward others in your everyday life. You'll need it to develop characters in your writing life.

Even in a short story, **time must pass** for characters to change believably.

➤ Develop your main character as someone with whom you would enjoy spending a great deal of time—because you will.

➤ Tell how a character feels, and you've given your readers a fact. Show how a character feels, and you've given your readers an emotion.

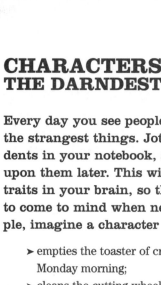

CHARACTERS DO THE DARNDEST THINGS

Every day you see people doing or saying the strangest things. Jot down these incidents in your notebook, and elaborate upon them later. This will log character traits in your brain, so they are more apt to come to mind when needed. For example, imagine a character who:

➤ empties the toaster of crumbs every Monday morning;

➤ cleans the cutting wheel on the electric can opener once a week because it's "the dirtiest quarter inch in your kitchen";

- ➤ visits a different card shop each day to read the greeting cards;
- ➤ names his son Sharon, after the steel mill town in Pennsylvania;
- ➤ tugs at one sleeve because that arm is slightly longer than the other;
- ➤ telephones her son to remind him again how difficult his birth was for her;
- ➤ stands on tiptoes in family photos to appear taller;
- ➤ vacuums the attic.

Who wants to write—or read—about ordinary characters? Make yours original by absorbing the people around you.

Well-drawn **characters carry** emotional and psychological **baggage**.

> Characters disdain in others what they cannot abide in themselves—just like people do.

In most stories, the antagonist writes the problem; the protagonist writes the resolution.

➤ The most difficult decisions for characters are those in which each alternative promises both good and bad outcomes.

➤ Characters' behavior follows a pattern: They feel, they think, they act—though sometimes they skip the second part.

➤ Readers will like a character for the character's strengths. Readers will embrace a character for the character's weaknesses.

➤ Your character's way of thinking, as well as the thoughts themselves, help to define your character. From time to time, let the reader sneak a peek into the character's thought process.

If you doesn't love your protagonist,
neither will the reader.

Mistakes, flaws, and contradictions make characters three dimensional.

➤ During dialogue and internal monologues, provide your characters with "stage business"—trivial but distinctive actions, e.g., adjusting the blinds, browsing through a magazine, or retying boot laces.

You, as the writer, must know exactly how each character feels, **even if the character doesn't.**

➤ Even the most cerebral of characters are at their most endearing when they act on the basis of emotion rather than intellect.

➤ You don't have to like every character you create. You shouldn't, in fact. But you must be awfully curious about them.

> Avoid thumbnail sketches of characters. Let readers come to know your characters gradually, just as in real life.

A character's physical appearance may not be important to the plot, but it is **always important** to the reader.

Still waters may run deep, but still characters **are just still.**

> In fiction there are no selfless acts: Even the most altruistic character acts as he or she must in order to feel good and to be at peace.

➤ Readers are interested in people: what happens to them, how they think and feel, what they do. Everything else is decorative.

➤ You may love your characters. You may hate your characters. But you may not feel indifferent toward your characters.

Create each character in your head, then give just enough information for the reader to do the same.

STORY STARTERS

Having trouble visualizing your characters? Choose one of these openings and continue the story. As the story evolves, so will the characters' traits and mannerisms.

When Sam Caligari visits his mother, she empties the refrigerator onto the kitchen table and announces each selection. She pushes each dish closer to her son's plate—just to make sure he sees it—until he eats some of everything.

Donald Quinn was born old. He clips the nails of his left hand every Monday evening, the right hand every Tuesday evening. Left toe nails on Wednesday, right toe nails on Thursday. He'll be able to skip next Tuesday.

Alicia Davies peddles her tricycle side by side with her dad's wheelchair. Each wears the other's smile, though she is fair-skinned and he is dark.

Be cruel to your characters. Push them until they absolutely **must take action**.

The writer must **know each character's ruling passion** and allow the reader to discover it.

> Characters who have lived well and fully before the story begins are more likely to grab the reader's interest.

When choosing a point-of-view character, ask yourself, **"Who is the reader supposed to be?"**

➤ Help the reader distinguish between your characters by showing not only what the characters own, but how they treat their possessions.

➤ Many readers identify so strongly with the point-of-view character that they will argue with other characters, even as they read.

➤ You should be able to answer any question about your main characters. By the end of the story, so should the reader.

➤ The reader should know the main characters well enough to carry on the storyline even after the story has ended.

Readers relate to characters who are trying to make their lives better—especially in the face of setbacks.

The more opinionated the characters, the more **potential for conflict.**

A character may or may not play fair, but she never argues fair.

> How your characters choose to
spend their time **shows their
true priorities.**

➤ Unlike people in real life, characters never just go
through the motions. Fictional characters always
act with purpose.

➤ In a phrase or two, identify each character's
defining persona—that which sets the character
apart and creates a mental image.

➤ Each character in a scene must want something. Otherwise, the character has no business appearing in the scene.

➤ Secondary characters work with or against the protagonist. There are no neutral characters.

A character's deeds will reveal who he is more powerfully than his words.

Each character makes his fictional
world a little better or a little poorer
for having been a part of it.

➤ The biggest challenges for a character include risking everything she has worked to achieve, especially love, and risking the lives of those she loves, especially children.

Imagine what a **cardboard character** would say or do. Now write something altogether different.

➤ Think of your characters as moving in a force field—being pulled this way and that as they move toward their respective goals.

➤ No character is altogether good nor altogether evil. Show the good guy's bad side and the bad guy's good side.

Secondary characters are the screw-
drivers of fiction: infinitely **versatile**
in putting things together.
—Nancy Kress, author of the Beggars Trilogy

The situation comes first. The characters—always flat
and unfeatured, to begin with—come next. Once these
things are fixed in my mind, I begin to narrate.
—Stephen King, author of *Carrie* and *It*

The words *hero* and *heroine* sound impossibly grand,
invoking wartime bravery and inhuman fortitude.
—Donald Maass, author and literary agent

We must have a weak spot or two in a character before
we can love it much.
—Oliver Wendell Holmes, Sr., poet and humorist

If your characters are having more fun than you are, **you're on the right track.**

➤ Your main character's ability to resolve problems should be hampered, but the task not made impossible, by his or her frailties.

➤ Through story events, allow your characters to discover in themselves the talents and strengths they need to resolve their problems.

In fiction as in real life, characters are **partly right and partly wrong** about most things.

➤ Just for fun—or for effect—name a character after a musical instrument or a piece of furniture or a fruit or a vegetable.

➤ Good characters have their weaknesses; evil characters have their strengths. And both have their reasons.

A character's greatest weakness, cast in different circumstances, becomes the character's greatest strength.

> How might your viewpoint character react to his or her reflection in a window or display case?

Characters take on different roles in different relationships, just as people do in life.

In developing your characters, comfort the afflicted and **afflict the comfortable.**

The worse things get for your hero or heroine, the sweeter the triumph for your readers.

➤ Most readers identify with the first character they encounter. Introduce your readers to the main character first and to the secondary characters later.

➤ Characters must be more starkly defined than people in real life. And their situations more threatening.

Plot gets readers involved; characterization makes them care.

➤ What might you find in your main character's trash can at work? The trash can at home? In the refrigerator? Glove compartment? Medicine cabinet, night stand, junk drawer? Pocket or purse?

➤ A character's living space should complement the character's personality, the way a bit of blue in a wall hanging picks up the blue in a bedspread or drape.

➤ The first few details that come to mind to describe a character may do for a start, but don't stop there. Keep picturing the character until you discover more vivid distinctions.

➤ Put your characters in a situation outside the present story. If they continue to interact, you know your characters.

Know the character, and you'll know the character's story.

In the best stories, the main character overcomes not only an adversary, but a **weakness of self** as well.

➤ To explore the depth of your lead character, ask another writer to interview you as that character, and record the interview.

Character traits are to **fiction** as caricatures are to **political cartoons.**

➤ You can learn a lot about a character by listening to the way the character talks about enemies—and even more from the way the character talks about friends.

➤ In fiction, as in real life, the last person to understand something is the first person to explain it to everybody else.

➤ During the writing process, give each main character a temporary name describing that character's primary feature.

➤ The most interesting situations are seldom what they seem to be, and the most interesting characters are seldom who they seem to be.

Repeat, with variations, your **character's identifying mannerisms.**

Every memorable character **has a wart**, of sorts.

DIALOGUE:

Reading Is a Lot Like Eavesdropping

Writing dialogue is simply giving a voice to **the characters that live inside of us.**

—Gloria Kempton, author and writing instructor

Once you use those quotation marks, it's not you the writer talking. It's you the writer listening.
> —Alberto Rios, author of *The Iguana Killer: Twelve Stories of the Heart*

The pen is the tongue of the mind.
> —Miguel de Cervantes, Spanish novelist, playwright, and poet

Literature is news that stays news.
> —Ezra Pound, poet and critic

Dialogue is the gas pedal of your story. Step on the pedal and the story speeds up.

➤ High-tension dialogue calls for fewer beats (less stage business). More beats will elongate a scene, as when characters get to know each other over dinner.

➤ Good dialogue is artfully concise.

> Characters are able to say things on the spur of the moment the way we wish we could in life.

Interludes of dialogue are to the novel as parks are to the city.

Skinny the narrative and **fatten the dialogue.**

➤ The first rule of dialogue: Give your characters something interesting to say.

➤ Dialogue creates white space on the page, making a book easier to read and more approachable.

Dialogue is conversation with the boring parts taken out.

LISTENING FOR GREAT DIALOGUE

You know more about writing dialogue than you think. After all, you listen to the dialogue of "characters" in your life all the time. You recognize when someone says something "out of character." You recognize when someone is putting on airs or talking down to you or affecting a false manner of speaking.

As Anne Lamott, author of *Bird by Bird*, advises, give yourself permission to experience the world as a writer. For example, carry a notebook with you, and write down bits of dialogue, especially if the manner of speech is unlike your own. Later, type your notes (without editing) into a dialogue file. The typing and transposing will engrain into your writerly brain a range of voices that will show up as distinctive character voices on paper.

In taking my order for breakfast one morning, a waitress mocked the menu by asking, "And how would you like those farm-fresh eggs?" Next she asked, "And what part of the pig would you like this morning?"

I could never hope to make up dialogue that would so economically reveal attitude and personality. I didn't have to. I paid attention and wrote it down.

Well-written **dialogue is efficient stuff:** It reveals character, lends realism, and advances the plot.

> Nothing is as dull or as useless as a dialogue of agreement.

In fiction, just as in real life, one-on-one dialogue works best.

➤ Rather than be clever in your spelling of a character's dialogue, be clever in your choice of words for the character's dialogue. In short, focus on diction, not dialect.

➤ Dialect is difficult to write and an imposition on the reader if executed poorly.

To get into the **flow of writing** dialogue, imagine what a close friend or relative would say in a given situation.

➤ Record and transcribe, verbatim, an everyday conversation. Compare it with well-written dialogue. Straight away, you'll see the difference.

➤ In writing dialogue, avoid chit-chat. Well-written dialogue only appears to reflect everyday speech.

Dialect is better created in the reader's imagination than **splattered on the page.**

STORY STARTERS
Having trouble with your dialogue? Choose one of these openings, each with a bit of dialogue. Let that bit of dialogue guide you in continuing the story. What else might this character say?

The last casserole Edda Maye Stoner brought me came with an apology. "The chicken just sort of walked through it," she said in a rusty voice. She handed me the still-warm dish through the driver's window. I knew she must be in awful pain.

The minister's been missing for three months now. "Even the best dog can't chase two rabbits at the same time," he liked to say. Some folks from the congregation, mostly Laddie and Sue, are keeping up the chapel, but no one has suggested we look for a new minister.

I had never noticed the discolorations on Sarah's face before, as if age were a spotting disease that had come on her while she was in the hospital. I leaned forward to tuck the sheet under her chin. One eye flew open. "I ain't dead yet."

➤ The main character's dialogue, if written well,
   becomes the reader's own words.

➤ Read your dialogue aloud. Note where your tongue
   trips. This is where your dialogue is most apt to be
   out of character.

Each character's dialogue
must serve a purpose—unlike
dialogue in real life.

➤ Many readers skip long narrative passages to get to the good stuff—what characters say and do to each other. Do the same as you write.

➤ In fiction, remember that one character never tells another what the latter already knows.

When you read your dialogue, listen for **cadence and rhythm and breathing.**

Creativity is the power
to connect the seemingly unconnected.
—William Plomer, poet, memoirist, novelist,
and short story writer

Writing ... is but a different name for conversation.
—Laurence Sterne, author of *Tristram Shandy*

All the information you need in a book can be put
in dialogue.
—Elmore Leonard, author of *Mr. Paradise* and *A Coyote's
in the House*

I think all writing is a disease. You can't stop it.
—William Carlos Williams, Pulitzer Prize-winning poet

Characters mention the weather **only if it is relevant.**

➤ When attributing dialogue, "said" is all that needs to be said.

Unlike real-life conversation, story dialogue never just passes the time of day.

➤ Characters rely less on nonverbal communication than we do in everyday life, so load your dialogue with the diction of emotion.

➤ The purpose of attribution is to let the reader know who is speaking, not how the speaker said it or what the speaker was feeling at the time.

WHOSE LINE IS IT?

Highlight all the dialogue by your lead character. Use a different color to highlight all the dialogue by the second most important character, another color for the third most important, and so on.

Note the proportion of highlighted material to unhighlighted material. Remember that readers love dialogue. Some readers even skip narration to get to it.

Also, the proportion of dialogue for each character should be in keeping with that character's importance, unless you have a character who is taciturn or loquacious.

Now read only the lead character's dialogue. Make sure the voice is consistent and distinctive. Do the same for each of the other major players. As a further test, eliminate all the dialogue attribution (he said, she said). You should be able to tell whose dialogue it is by the speaker's diction and syntax.

Dialogue is the clearest way of signaling **a change in a relationship.**

➤ Characters must have a reason to say what they say—something beyond the writer's need to convey information.

➤ Avoid trendy speech in dialogue. By the time the story is published, the catchphrase may no longer be trendy, and your work will date itself quickly.

➤ Writing dialogue is great fun! You are allowed to break the rules of grammar, and you get to say anything you want under the guise of character.

In everyday life, we dull the edges of our conversations. In writing, we hone the edge.

Avoid using adverbs to attribute dialogue. Well-written dialogue will speak for itself.

➤ Clichés may be used in dialogue to reveal character, but never in narration.

➤ If you need an adverb to describe how someone said something, the dialogue has failed.

Carry a notepad to **write down the good stuff** as soon as you overhear it.

Reading good dialogue **is a lot like eaves-dropping.** No wonder readers love it!

PLOT:

Get Your Character Out of the Tree

Surely it was time someone invented a new plot, **or that the author came out from the bushes.**

—Virginia Woolf, author of *A Room of One's Own* and *Orlando*

Persons attempting to find a motive in this narrative will be prosecuted; persons attempting to find a moral in it will be banished; persons attempting to find a plot in it will be shot.

—Mark Twain, author of *Tom Sawyer*

If I didn't know the ending of a story, I wouldn't begin. I always write my last line, my last paragraph, my last page first.

—Katherine Anne Porter, Pulitzer Prize-winning author of *Collected Short Stories of Katherine Anne Porter*

Good fiction begins in real life, but it **doesn't stay long.**

➤ In your everyday life, avoid trouble. In your writing life, revel in it.

➤ There is nothing quite so slippery as an undeveloped story idea.

HOW TO BEGIN WRITING A STORY

In our everyday conversations, we begin a story with the most exciting part, then back up to fill in the details. The same is true in good writing. Begin with the exciting part, then back up to fill in the details.

To get started, write whatever you feel most strongly about or the part of the story you most want to write. This is your emotional trigger. Write forward and backward from your starting point. Don't be concerned with what belongs or doesn't belong. Don't be concerned with the order in which the different parts should be presented. Rewriting and editing come later. In writing the story, you will discover how the story should begin for the reader.

Sometimes the emotional trigger is not clear—you just have a vague desire to write about something that's on your mind. In that case, start with whatever you have—a bit of dialogue, a particular setting, a distinctive character, a what-if question or an action scene.

The point is to begin. What you write may seem dull or muddy or just plain dumb. No matter. Sometimes we need to write our way through the lousy stuff to get to the good stuff. So begin.

➤ Plotting is simple. Just ask, "What could possibly go wrong?"

➤ Well-constructed plots seem inevitable. The story just couldn't have turned out any differently, even if there are numerous twists and an unexpected ending.

Plot requires more than a mere sequence of events; it requires a causal sequence of events.

> Story is what happens. Plot is how and why.

If the good guy or the bad guy can just walk away, **there is no story.**

Plotting is like a child at play: **Skip as much as possible.**

Plotting is not only what to tell, but **when to tell it.**

➤ Things don't just happen in fiction. What happens must grow out of the characters' wants and resources.

➤ In fiction, everything happens for a reason. (Some people believe this is true in real life, too.)

STORY STARTERS

Do characters spring from plot or does plot flow from characters? Doesn't matter. Use whatever approach works best for you. As author Marshall J. Cook says, "There is no wrong way to do it." So choose one of these openings, and show us what happens next.

First thing they did was shoot the dog. I knew right off there was gonna be real trouble this time.

While waiting to be seated, the distinguished-looking man whispered something to his much-younger companion. She quickly fluffed her hair with her fingers, first on one side and then on the other, to hide the bright pink of her ears.

Perched on the edge of the couch in his apartment, she approved of the coordinated furnishings, the area rugs, the accent pieces. But it was the complementary colors in the wall hangings that decided the matter.

➤ The protagonist must resolve the story's major conflict through willful choices and actions, not by an act of nature or the intervention of other characters.

➤ The more obstacles the protagonist must overcome, the better the story—and the better readers will like it, especially if the obstacles are varied and increasingly difficult.

In fiction, just as in life, **everything relates to everything**, only more so.

ACTING OUT

Writing is a lot like acting, except the writer gets to play all the roles. Whether your writing space is a room of your own, a wooded glen at a writers' retreat, or a kitchen nook, transpose that space into a stage for whatever scene you are working on. Speak all the characters' lines in full thunder or *sotto voce*, take action with or against other characters, and move about your stage. Become each of your characters.

You'll be amazed at what the characters reveal about themselves through dialogue, actions, and gestures. As a writer, you are part director, part scribe.

➤ The best plot developments—and the most difficult choices for characters—arise when there are good and bad aspects to every option.

Plots always **answer the questions** they pose.

In a strong plot, **more than one thing** is always going on.

> Motive is the linchpin between character and plot. Characters' motives drive the action.

A single well-cast scene **will reveal more** than an encyclopedia of narration.

➤ The climax occurs when the main character is up against the wall and must make a crucial decision. At that moment, the character's most important value is defined.

You should be able to **state the purpose** of each scene in ten words or less.

➤ Rather than anguish over the next development in your story, play with several—until one is more fun to play with than all the others.

➤ Before falling asleep at night, review everything you know about a plot problem—without trying to resolve it. When you wake, you may have the solution.

> Each scene should be a microcosm of the story whole: A problem is introduced, heightened, and resolved. In other words, something must change.

Never resolve one conflict **before presenting another.**

Each major scene should include a ticking clock (in a figurative sense). The protagonist **must do something** ... right now!

> There are three themes in most fiction: Life is a struggle, humans are resilient, and effort will triumph.

For a writer, constructing the background material can be so much fun that **it's mistaken for writing.**

—Ansen Dibell, author of *Plot*

Why did you put so much suffering in the world? And God answers, Because it makes a better story.

—Stanley Elkin, author of *The Living End*

You don't have to be able to outline a plot if you have a reasonably long life expectancy.

—Tony Hillerman, author of *The Wailing Wind* and *Skeleton Man*

You can always count on a murderer for a fancy prose style.

—Vladimir Nabokov, author of *Lolita* and *Pale Fire*

Plots are found as theme unfolds
to the writer. Themes are found as
plot unfolds to the reader.

➤ A sex scene, like any other scene, must reveal
  character and advance the plot.

➤ Readers are apt to believe the sex scenes are autobi-
  ographical, so flatter yourself.

> Plots are condensed life. Themes are evaporated life.

If you cannot summarize your story in a sentence, you may be **writing more than one story.**

➤ In a well-written story, the reader will act out the big scenes moment by moment.

➤ The first idea that occurs to you for resolving a plot problem will be the first to occur to the reader as well. So think again.

Until you decide the story is finished, plot is tentative.

There are three elements to every plot: Get your character up a tree. Put tigers under the tree. **Get your character out of the tree.**

FICTION TECHNIQUES:

Dead Men Tell No Tales

The idea of a novel **should stir your blood.**

—Pat Conroy, author of *My Losing Season* and
The Great Santini

Writers almost always write best what they know, and
sometimes they do it by staying where they know it. But
not for safety's sake.

—Eudora Welty, Pulitzer Prize-winning author of
The Optimist's Daughter

We're past the age of heroes and hero kings. If we can't
make up stories about ordinary people, who can we make
them up about.

—John Updike, Pulitzer Prize-winning author of *Rabbit Is Rich*
and *Rabbit at Rest*

➤ Start in the middle of things. Open every story with an unwanted pregnancy, so to speak.

➤ Savvy real estate agents lead prospective buyers into a house through its most engaging aspect, just as writers should lead readers into a story. In short, enter through the sun porch, not the garage.

The short rule for research:
Pay attention and jot everything down.

The best openings cause readers to pose questions to which they simply **must find out the answers.**

➤ The expanded rules for research: Smell the flowers and the water treatment plant. Touch the underside of everything. Stare at ordinary people. Alternate putting your finger in one ear then the other. Open your mouth only to taste something.

Write the first draft as fast as you can.

> Some writers, unable to get their short fiction published, decide to write a novel instead. This is like deciding to build a house because the tool shed you built fell apart.

Begin with conflict rather than description.

In drawing fiction from real life, play **fast and loose** with the facts that you may write sure and well of the truth.

➤ Scribble down an idea when it first occurs to you. Even if you remember it later, the language in which you convey it will never again be as fresh and alive.

A well-crafted opening should
"put a worry on a body."

➤ The beginning of a story is the writer's first chance
to make a good impression, and the ending is the
writer's last chance to make a lasting impression.

➤ Here's a quick test for your story's opening: If you
were waiting in line at the checkout stand and you
read the first few paragraphs of the story, would
you buy the magazine?

THE NAME GAME

Some writers insist they cannot proceed until they have named their lead characters. One option is to borrow the names of people who remind you of your fictional characters, just to get on with the writing.

At some point, appropriate names may spring from the writing or from serendipity. If you get stuck, you might pair one part of a real-life name with part of another real-life name. Or choose a relevant synonym or antonym. Or pick a name the way you might pick a computer password, by choosing some object from your writ-

ing environment. Remember that if a
name is difficult to read aloud, it's difficult
to read silently.

What's in a name? Certainly not
enough to keep you from writing.

In early scenes, **introduce the settings** in which big scenes will occur later.

➤ Think of your writing as a series of double doors opening inward, drawing the reader ever deeper into the story.

Setting is a supporting character—interacting with other characters to **advance the storyline.**

➤ Actors ask of the director, "What is my motivation in this scene?" Characters ask the same of the writer.

➤ To heighten dramatic tension, locate the scene at a place of high tension—or just the opposite.

➤ A change in setting is to writing as eerie music is to suspense movies: a signal that something important is about to happen.

➤ In real life, most "scenes" don't change much of anything. In fiction, every scene changes something.

Of every scene the writer must ask,
"What's at stake?"

Paint the setting with broad strokes; **add detail** from time to time.

STORY STARTERS

Ready to try your hand at developing and expanding your writing techniques? Choose one of these openings and continue the story. Have fun with it. Indulge your imagination.

The old man fumbled for his insurance cards. His wallet, a long ago gift from his son who had cut and sewn the leather together as a Boy Scout project, was falling apart.

He shifted his weight from one foot to the other, trying to find some island of comfort between the pain in his left ankle and the pain in his right knee. Even the mirror was soiled in her dingy bathroom.

She relished the casual din of the slot machines. It bathed and comforted her, like the familiar, slightly sweet scent of the recycled air. She swiveled on her barstool and flipped the first of the evening's quarters onto the carpeted floor.

> In a well-crafted story, the reader knows life will never again be the same for the main character. Perhaps, the same will be true of the reader's life.

In life, there is **no authorial voice-over** announcing people's motives and emotions. Nor should there be in fiction.

Think of your story as if **each scene were to be illustrated,** for that is exactly what the reader does.

> Most of today's readers demand immediate gratification. The writer must pose and resolve one conflict after another en route to resolving the main story problem.

Provide enough detail to stimulate the reader's imagination, then get out of the way.

➤ Read a scene in any well-written story. Visualize it. Now read the passage again. Note all the details left out by the writer—but supplied by your imagination.

➤ To keep readers revved up, make things worse for your main character (preferably much worse) before things get better.

Leave the histrionics for the soap-operas and melodramas. Put the emotion in your verbs.

➤ Readers hold each scene in suspended animation, reshaping the scene as details are revealed. To painstakingly set up each scene is to distrust the reader.

➤ Scenes engage the reader by providing immediacy. Narration varies the rhythm, allowing the reader to breathe between scenes.

➤ If you get everything else wrong, but move the reader with your emotion, you have succeeded.

➤ Conflict among choices of the mind may intrigue the reader. Conflict among choices of the heart will involve the reader.

Rule of thumb: Your main character should fail at least twice to resolve the story problem, then succeed.

THE NAME GAME REVISITED

Writers often name their characters so as to reflect a personality trait. In *Fugitive Nights*, Joseph Wambaugh carries the technique a step further. We are introduced to a retired drug cop, Jack Graves, whose state of mind has been damaged by his accidental shooting of a child in the line of duty.

Jack Graves is, indeed, of a grave demeanor. In the course of events, we learn about Jack Graves' physical appearance, life style, and mannerisms. But the essence of Jack Graves is communicated most clearly by the simple repetition of his full name. Every time Jack Graves is referred to, every time Jack Graves speaks a line, we are given both his first and last name. And Jack Graves is the only character referred to in this way. Wambaugh's technique is subtle—and effective.

Are any of your characters' names worth repeating?

To create a fast-read, write the entire story **as if it were only 150 words.**

➤ The writer owns the black marks on the page. The reader owns the white space. Respect the reader's property rights.

The reader gets to know everything the point-of-view character knows.

➤ In real life, events of the day sometimes foreshadow future developments. In fiction, they always do.

➤ Unless something relevant happens in transit, don't burden the reader with descriptions of how characters get from one place to another.

➤ During moments of high conflict or emotional intensity, our powers of observation are heightened, our mental camera records everything in detail and presents the scene in slow motion. The same is true in fiction.

➤ Try writing a story as an "inverted pyramid." Facts first, then elaboration.

Switching from past tense to present tense is the equivalent of using slow-motion in a movie.

> Both the protagonist and the antagonist must be allowed to use their talents and resources fully to try to get what they want.

To broaden your skills, write as if for a person who has **never been gifted with sight.**

Readers love good secrets. Allow readers to **tease the secrets** out of your characters.

➤ Most readers won't notice if you change point of view a hundred times—but they will notice the book doesn't feel right.

➤ If you school yourself, you will learn technique layer by layer until you are sagging with the stuff. Then one day you will break free of it, and start writing naturally.

The primary rule of good
story-telling: **Get on with it!**

Readers insist that **everything tie together in a novel** precisely because things rarely do so in real life.

➤ When you first learn a writing technique, practice it at every turn. Then forget it. It will resurface in subsequent writing, unbidden, when you need it.

➤ If you shift point-of-view or alter time sequences or employ dialect or use esoteric language or do anything that makes the story more difficult to read, be sure you gain more than you lose.

I write from the **worm's eye point of view.**

—Ernie Pyle, Pulitzer Prize-winning journalist

And that is all there is to good writing, putting down on the paper words which dance and weep and make love and fight and kiss and perform miracles.

—Gertrude Stein, author of *The Making of Americans*

Writing a novel is like driving at night. You can see ahead only as far as your headlights, but you can make the whole trip that way.

—E. L. Doctorow, author of *Billy Bathgate* and *City of God*

If a flashback runs on too long or isn't wholly relevant, **it becomes a flopback.**

> Internal monologues should be about as long as the character's nose.

> A simple rule for titles: Get the reader interested, then make the title mean something different by the end of the story.

When your novel **sags in the middle,** it develops a **plot-belly.**

Choose as your point-of-view character the person **most at risk** in the story.

➤ Create a character readers have never met but hope they might; involve the character in a conflict readers hope never to encounter; enable the character to resolve the conflict; and allow readers to discover truth in the process. Seems simple enough.

➤ Writing in the first-person point of view is often a good choice for a first draft, but usually a lousy choice for a final draft.

➤ If readers don't like the ending of your book, they will hate the whole book.

When the writer stops to describe something, the reader stops, too.

Dead men tell no tales, except in forensics. And point-of-view characters never die.

STYLE:
Write Against the Wind

We must constantly ask if our words are meaning what they say, and **saying what we mean.**

—Sheridan Baker, author of *The Practical Stylist*

The original writer is not one who imitates nobody, but one whom nobody can imitate.

—François René de Chateaubriand, author of *Atala* and *The Genius of Christianity*

The search for style is a fool's errand: You have it, whatever it is, from the day you put the first word on a page.

—Michael Seidman, author of *Fiction: The Art and Craft of Writing and Getting Published*

Overwriting is a date only with yourself.

—Julie Checkoway, editor of *Creating Fiction*

- Whisper your observations onto the page.

- The writer works hard so that the reader doesn't have to.

In good fiction, **truth is seldom implied**, but rather inferred.

Handle your words as carefully as you handle your money.

If a piece is really well written, no one notices the writing.

➤ You know your work is good when readers say, "Oh, I could have written that!"

➤ It's okay for a character to show off. It's not okay for a writer to show off.

➤ In fiction, as in life, what is suggested is far more powerful than what is revealed.

DIALOGUE TAGS
REVEAL LAZY WRITING

Dialogue tags are adverbs used to tell the reader how a line of dialogue is delivered, like *she said sincerely* or *he asked pleadingly*, and they're nothing more than crutches.

Sure, it's easier to add an adverb than to write a good line of dialogue. But it's worth the effort to let the character's words express intent and emotion, as in this line from Mitch Albom's *The Five People You Meet in Heaven*, "Kid, I never been anywhere I wasn't shipped to with a rifle."

An exception favoring the use of dialogue tags occurs when a line is delivered in an uncommon or unexpected manner. "I love you with every fiber of my being," he said sarcastically. But even that example would be better rendered without the tag, perhaps in her response, "I can do without your dimwit sarcasm."

Dialogue tags? Nah, you don't need those crutches.

➤ Every fiction writer should compose poetry; it sharpens imagery and disciplines diction.

➤ The diction required to write children's stories is akin to that required to write poetry.

➤ Find the confidence to write simply.

Never make the reader aware that he or she is being told a story.

> If the reader
> becomes
> aware of style
> or technique,
> the writer is
> getting in
> the way.

Talent is a matter
of genetics. Style is
**a matter of
examined
practice.**

Develop **an eye for detail.** And an ear. And a nose. And a taste and feel, as well.

➤ Diction is the currency of writing. It is the medium of exchange and evidence of literary worth.

Every stinking word you write evokes a particular response. Like "stinking" in the previous sentence.

➤ Writing is making the same mistake over and over until you learn to not make that particular mistake anymore.

➤ Write close to the bone.

➤ Show truth as if your character had just discovered it. Show emotion as if your character had just invented it.

➤ If you manage to move yourself as you write, whether to laughter or to tears, to anguish or to joy, chances are your work also will move the reader.

A crisp analogy will define an image more sharply than extended prose—and with greater economy.

STORY STARTERS

Here's an opportunity to try writing in a different style. Choose one of these openings and continue the story in the same style. If the style drifts into something altogether your own, rejoice!

She pushed her coffee mug away, then dragged it closer. Her eyes flitted to the window, to the rim of the booth near my shoulder, to the salad bar over my other shoulder, to the edge of our table, and finally alighted on me like tandem butterflies.

I am afraid of being hauled away in front of my wife and neighbors. I am afraid it will not be the police who come for me. I am afraid of not dying from the first beating.

You mow a ten-foot swath on each side of the dirt road. All along your frontage, nearly a quarter of a mile. You do it because you like the way it looks. It makes no sense, like Alice dying young from those lumps growing inside her.

In writing, **better too little than too much**— except for return postage.

> The more constrained a writer is by word count, the better the writing.

Early drafts are generous; polished drafts are stingy.

➤ Economy renders significance.

➤ Less is more. Much less is much more.

➤ Never waste your reader's time.

The tombstone engraver is paid by the letter; the writer is not.

➤ "To be" and all her kin sloth about—the laziest verb family in the land. Choose a verb that works harder.

➤ "If in doubt, leave it out." It works for commas and modifiers. It works for phrases, sentences, and paragraphs. Heck, it works for whole chapters.

➤ Interest Level equals Word Count divided by New Information.

➤ Writers write long when they haven't taken the time to write short.

Think of your writing as a house before moving day. You have to get rid of the clutter.

OFFER YOUR READERS A COLORING BOOK

Think of your story as a coloring book, with characters and scenes presented only in outline. As the story unfolds, the reader colors each scene based on his or her knowledge and experience, creating a personal rendering of the story. The details you provide influence the reader's choice of crayons, especially in genre fiction.

Consider the opening of Dean Koontz' *The Face of Fear*:

> Wary, not actually expecting trouble, but prepared for it, he parked his car across the street from the four-story brownstone apartment

house. When he switched off the engine, he heard a siren wail in the street behind him.

Koontz mentions the brownstone apartment house, but did you feel the gray and the other somber colors? Or did you feel the sunshine splashing everything with vivid colors? You colored the scene in keeping with your knowledge and experiences.

When you write your story, offer your readers a coloring book ... and plenty of crayons.

Simple language **doesn't mean simple-minded.** It means you are apt to be read.

➤ You need to know a lot of words to be a writer. But not the ten-dollar words. Instead, get to know the ten-cent words really well.

➤ Like flowering plants, words show best when arranged among others of complement and contrast.

Nouns and verbs are **movers and shakers**— the power players of language.

Use a thesaurus, if you must, to remind yourself of the **right word,** but not to impose one.

> There are no adverbs in real life.

➤ Writers are more likely to fail for knowing too many words than too few.

Every paragraph, every sentence, every word must **carry its weight**, must do a job.

Anything that is written to please the author **is worthless.**

—Blaise Pascal, French mathematician, physicist, and religious philosopher

Straightening out grammar and syntax is not the be-all and end-all of writing. But you need a command of language as much as you need a commanding idea.

—Karen Elizabeth Gordon, author of *Sin and Syntax*

The finest language is mostly made up of simple unimposing words.

—George Eliot, author of *Middlemarch*

Any authentic creation is a gift to the future.

—Albert Camus, author of *The Stranger* and *The Plague*

Put the qualifiers up front. End each sentence with a PUNCH.

➤ Don't take yourself too seriously. As in acting, just say the line—speak the words onto the page.

➤ Create as does a child, without concern for what others may think or whether it's been done before.

Strive not to create good writing but good reading.

➤ If you write fiction by the rules, you might as well be writing about how to change a tire.

➤ A story's real length is determined by how long it feels to the reader.

> **Beware the Land of the Ing's!**

Move the verb **as far forward as possible.** It enlivens your writing, you see.

"Better safe than sorry" in living. **"Safe is sorry" in writing.**

➤ Take risks in your writing. If not there, where?

➤ Structure your sentences and paragraphs so as to allow the reader to breathe—unless you intend for the reader to become breathless.

➤ One's style, be it pedantic, engaging, or boorish, has about the same effect in writing as in conversation.

For every rule of thumb, there is always an insolent pinky finger that does its own thing.

Write against the wind.

VOICE:
Quit Trying to Be Writerly

Every compulsion is put upon writers to become **safe, polite, obedient, and sterile.**

—Sinclair Lewis, Nobel Prize-winning author

The most original authors are not so because they advance what is new, but because they put what they have to say as if it had never been said before.

—Johann Wolfgang von Goethe, poet, novelist, and playwright

When we are alone reading, each of us hears a little voice in our heads, and this is the voice of the writer speaking to us.

—Mike Magnuson, author of *Heft on Wheels*

What is written without effort is read without pleasure.

—Samuel Johnson, author and editor

> Most readers will never hear the writer's speaking voice. They will hear the writer's voice as it emerges from the page.

A writer must have something to say and **a voice with which to say it.**

Voice rings true when it **reflects aspects** of the writer's self.

➤ The secret to getting published is to write something good. The key to writing something good is to cultivate a distinctive voice.

➤ Voice refers to the way a writer speaks to the reader. Voice is neither learned nor trained. Voice evolves.

A NEW REALITY

Suspending disbelief refers to the reader's willingness to accept a reality created by the writer. It's a state of mind, a readiness to believe in the improbable, even the impossible.

You can reinforce your reader's willingness to suspend disbelief by presenting consistent characters, realistic dialogue, and plausible action. And one thing more: Write with emotion in a voice the reader finds altogether believable.

Write what you care about, and you will likely move your reader to suspend disbelief and enter your world of creation.

A writer's voice and style are redefined with each new work according to the **needs of the work.**

> Stay true to your voice throughout the writing of your book. If you break with your voice, the book dies.

Discover an emotional truth within yourself. Present it to your readers. **Therein lies your voice.**

➤ To discover your voice, write as if your only reader is an intelligent but uninformed friend, an old friend whom you trust.

➤ Read the annual "best of" anthologies. Some technique will seep through, but mostly you'll be liberated to discover your own voice.

I have to believe I'm the only one who can tell this tale.

—Issac Bashevis Singer, author of *Zlateh the Goat and Other Stories*

If I had to put up a fight [with an editor], it would be over voice, not over advances and time frames.

—Jennifer Crusie, author of *Manhunting* and *What the Lady Wants*

Because they're reading in the first person, readers associate with the voice. They develop an understanding that they might have been this person if they had lived this history.

—Carole Maso, author of *Ghost Dance* and *Break Every Rule: Essays*

> Even if you make no conscious effort to discover your voice, you cannot escape offering a voice.

The real challenge is not for a you to find you voice, but to **choose the voice most appropriate** to the material.

A writer is most apt to **discover** a true voice when not as concerned with writing for publication as with writing to be read.

➤ Trust your instincts. Trust your observations. Trust your judgments. Trust your voice.

STORY STARTERS

Having trouble discovering your voice? Choose one of these openings, and continue the story. At first, try to sustain the voice presented in the opening, but feel free to develop a unique voice as you continue writing.

In the hour before first light, a monster truck screams along a two-lane blacktop toward the town of Pembroke, Ohio. Ahead, though not yet reflected in the truck's headlights, an Amish buggy also moves toward Pembroke. Its lone occupant, a young woman in a business suit, hears the rumble before she sees the truck.

Bob-Bob's face was on fire. He staggered away from the flames, eyes shut tight, and stumbled over a remnant of the barn's concrete floor. He sprawled onto the grass and slapped his face with both hands.

I saw only half her face, and only half a feint smile, as Celia eased the door closed. My treasured French coffee press, left sitting on the kitchen counter, popped into my head. But like so much else, I let it go.

Your voice won't likely ring true
until you have **accepted yourself
as a writer.**

➤ Voice is often the first thing new writers edit from
their work, and the most difficult to recapture.

➤ Voice is a reflection of the writer's personality. More
exactly, voice is a reflection of the personality a
writer must sustain for a particular piece of writing.

Voice arises when the writer **quits trying to be writerly.**

ABOUT THE AUTHOR

Paul Raymond Martin has published more than three hundred stories, poems, and articles. He is the author of *Writer's Little Instruction Book: Inspiration & Motivation*, *Writer's Little Instruction Book: Craft & Technique*, and *Writer's Little Instruction Book: Getting Published*, all from Writer's Digest Books.

Paul lives on a seventy-acre farm in northwestern Pennsylvania, where he leases the fields to a neighboring farmer. When he's not writing, Paul likes to play in the dirt and raise wormy apples.